WARRIOR

WARRIOR

GARY EDWERD MARRUFFO

iUniverse, Inc.
Bloomington

WARRIOR

iUniverse books may be ordered through booksellers or by contacting:

iUniverse
1663 Liberty Drive
Bloomington, IN 47403
www.iuniverse.com
1-800-Authors (1-800-288-4677)

ISBN: 978-1-4620-5075-8 (sc)
ISBN: 978-1-4620-5076-5 (ebk)

Printed in the United States of America

iUniverse rev. date: 10/12/2011

DEDICATION

I dedicate this story to all the people in America . . . to all the different races and all the different beliefs and religions. The way I look at it is that we are all here together and we will always be together. Nothing will ever change that. We have to accept this. We have all had wrong done to us in our life, to our race or way of living, whether in the past or now in our present. The point is if Indians can forgive then who has the right not to, I didn't write this story to change anybody but to inspire you to be who you are. You are your culture. Be proud of who you are and no one shall interfere. For they are who they are in their culture . . . one big costume party! Feel free to be your culture, your roots, and have fun because that's who you are.

Much love, one love, America!

Gary Marruffo

PREFACE

I wrote this story because of the great anger and hatred I had towards the white people for what unspeakable things they have done to my people. I know that it is ludicrous to think I could take on all the white people by myself and because of the great numbers of traitors. That if I wanted to engage in such actions it would be only a matter of time before I would be betrayed by my own people for disturbing the peace. I felt betrayed and hurt that people could go on living there lives with no regard to America's history because of my great love for God. I know he is a righteous God and if he loved me like I loved him, he would not allow me to be so hurt without making it right. So I started thinking how God would make this right, and the story of warrior unfolded. I started to think of the love of God and love that great is understanding . . . and understanding is forgiving and forgiving is divine . . . and divine is God. No matter how much anger and hatred I had, I know I would give it up just to be a part of God. We can't go forwards without forgiving, and if Indians can forgive, then who has the right to question that? Last, but not least, I wrote this story because I hate and can't stand racism and prejudice and will see it deceased that is worth dying for.

WARRIOR

Once upon a time there was an Indian warrior who loved his family. His way of life and was looking forward to being a grandfather of many. As a child he was more observant than other children. He would rather watch the elders of the tribe interact than' to go off and play with the other children. The elders of the tribe said he was a old spirit from the past. Instead of playing with the children he would just stay with the elders. The others would say, "Why don't you go play with the other children" But he just wouldn't. Then one day he was approached by a woman who did not greet him with a smile, but a tug on the arm and began dragging him to the place where the children were playing saying to him, "What is wrong with you? What is your problem? Are you weird or something?" leaving him among the other children. Young warrior did not think any of their games were interesting. He thought what they were doing was pointless. There he would sit on a rock and watch the children play. After the day had come to an end, he would follow them back to camp. Everyday the woman would be there and look at him and pointed towards the children as they played. Young warrior would put his head down and follow the children. He would go sit down on the same rock and watch the children play, thinking about what the elders were doing. He would think of what fun things he could be learning and he thought:

"Why should he be here doing something he thought was pointless? He put his head down and started to cry. The chief of the tribe used to like to watch the children play. He saw the young boy crying on the rock. The chief went to the young boy and said, "Why are you crying and why are you not playing with the other children?" The boy looked up at the chief and said "I just don't find playing fun. It's pointless." He said he would rather be back with the elders learning something fun and doing something that is not pointless. The chief smiled at the boy and said, "Well . . . why don't you go back to camp?" The boy started telling the chief about the woman who everyday would make him go play with the other children. The chief reached for the boy and pulled him on his horse. They started off to camp. The chief said to the boy, "Show me the woman." After searching the area, he pointed out and said, "That's her." The chief called to her and said, "Why were you bothering this young boy?" She said, "I thought a young boy should be playing with the other children, and thought it strange that a young boy like him didn't want to play with the other children." I thought by forcing him to go play would help him." The chief said, "He does not like to play with the other children."He is an old spirit from the past, so there will be no more of this." The woman said, "I understand and I will stop him no more." The young warrior smiled, got off the chiefs horse, and ran towards the people in the camp. He saw a woman making a basket and he sat down to watch her. With a grateful heart, and a smile on his face; he learned how to make a basket that day. He thought to himself: "How fun it is to learn!" And he was pleased. The next day and everyday after he would learn something new. The boy was five summers old. He would collect firewood for the older people of the tribe who could no longer get it for themselves. He learned to do one thing that made him proud and that was to burn sage. He offered up prayers to great grandfather spirit in the sky. He loved to pray. One thing that used to happen to him as a child, is he used to have dreams. Nightmares while he slept. One night he had a dream of pale people, people of no color, coming to his land with big canoes having a different lifestyle and way of life that he did not like. He did not know what his dream meant but always woke up feeling unpleasant, and weary. He would go to the chief and tell him of his dream, he would ask him to interpret the dream but every time he did the chief would just bow his head and not want to talk about it. He would bid the young warrior to forget it and not talk about it again.the boy did not understand why the chief did not wont to talk about the dream. So the young warrior went to the other wise men in the tribe, shared the dream with them; and asked them the meaning of the dream. All they would do is laugh and say that this dream you had is very interesting and you have a great imagination, but it means nothing because everyone in the world is like us. this is it we are the world

Now the young warrior was growing up. He was now sixteen years old. One day he went riding his horse on the prairie. There were many nice places, but his favorite place was upon a hill, where he loved to watch the sunset. He went everyday for many seasons of his young life. One day he rode to what he called Sunset

Hill and saw a person on a horse on the top of the hill. He wondered who it was, so he began riding towards the person. To his surprise it was a girl. A very beautiful girl, the prettiest one he has ever seen in his life. When they first looked into each other eyes, it was love at first sight.

"Hi, what is your name?"

"My name is Turquoise. What is your name?"

"My name is Warrior. How long have you been coming here?" said warrior

"Since I was thirteen," she said.

Warrior said, "Me too, but why haven't I ever seen you before?"

Turquoise was surprised that they had never seen each other before. She thought to herself because see did not come every day maybe it could be that when you came to see sunsets she did not and when see came you didn't come could it be that it was meant to be Warrior said, "It was meant to be." He smiled. He was glad that they finally met for the first time and did not want one more day to go by without them meeting each other. He thought to himself:

"Thank you great grandfather spirit for this day." They didn't stop talking to each other. They never broke eye contact. They didn't even notice that the sun was setting before them.

It was getting dark. They were both glad to have met each other and promised to meet again the next day. They both seemed to be happy and could not stop smiling at each other. They said good night to each other and went home. When warrior got home, he went to his bed. He laid there looking up with a smile on his face. He remembered that he didn't even ask Turquoise where she lived or what tribe she was from. He wondered if she would be safe on her way back home since it was getting dark. He hoped she was safe. He got up on his knees and lit a piece of sage and blew it out. He said a prayer, "Great grandfather spirit. Please watch over

Turquoise on her way home so that we can see each other tomorrow. Thank you great grandfather spirit." Then he let the sage burn out. He felt good and at peace. He laid back down and with a smile on his face he went to sleep. He had no dreams.

That night he slept in peace.

When he woke up the next day, he said to himself that that was the best sleep that he had ever had. He was pleased and excited. He thought: "It's a long time until sunset. He said to himself: "In order to make the day go by faster and to keep from thinking too much of Turquoise, he would keep busy." So he started working, doing everything that he could think of. He collected firewood for the elders who could no longer collect it for themselves. He thought the more work he did, the less he would think of Turquoise. But he was wrong. She would not leave his thoughts. He thought of her the whole day, even though he was busy and working hard. He thought that the day would not come to a end. Then finally the day did come to a end. He was glad and that finally he could get ready to go see Turquoise. He went and jumped in the river to clean up. He got ready then jumped on his horse and headed out to Sunset

Hill. When he got there, she wasn't there. He thought that she was not coming. He started to feel sad.

Then he saw her come from over the hill. He was happy to see her.

He smiled and waited for her. She was coming to him. As she approached him, he smiled at her. She was smiling back at him.

He said, "Hi. It's good to see you." She said, "It's nice to see you, too." He told her how he couldn't stop thinking about her all day and that when he got home he said a prayer for her that she would be safe on the journey home. She smiled and said that the whole way home, the wise old owl followed her. She said that she knew that someone was praying for her and that she thought that it was her parents. She was surprised that it was Warrior. She said,

"Thank you for your prayers. I arrived home safe with a feeling of great peace." They sat there and talked until it got dark once again.

They didn't even notice that the sunset had come and gone. They talked about where they lived and about each other's tribe, especially how different their tribes were. Neither of them ever knew their tribes were sworn enemies. Not even at this moment were they aware of what conflict could arise out of their affection.

It was time to start heading back home. It was getting dark. They agreed to meet each other back the same time the next day. They left the same time as the day before. When Warrior arrived home, he said another prayer for her and went to sleep. Once again he didn't dream and slept with great peace. When he awoke the next day, he went to the chief to tell him about the Indian girl and her tribe.the chief said she belongs to the Apache tribe the chief, said to the young warrior. "Be careful. The tribe that she's from doesn't get along with us. We've been at war with each other for many years. They will kill us and we will protect ourself from them. We don't go to their territories and they don't come to ours.

That's the only peace we have with each other. So I tell you not to see her anymore." The young warrior did not care. It did not even bother him.

Just before sunset, he set out to go see her. This time when he got there, she was waiting for him. She was not smiling. She looked sad. She said that she had told her mom about Warrior and about his tribe. She said, "Our tribes are enemies and they forbid me to see you ever again." The young warrior said, "The hell with them! I do not care what they say. I am going to keep seeing you.

Will you keep seeing me?" She said, "I don't care either. I will keep seeing you." They were very happy and laughed and smiled at each other. They promised that they would not talk about each other to their tribes anymore and they never did from that day on.

They met each other the next day and everyday after. They would not even wait for the sunset. They would meet in the mornings and they would spend everyday together. They were falling in love. Both Turquoise's and Warrior's parents and some of the people from their tribes would wonder where they went everyday. But they both said they were spending time with the great grandfather spirit. Their parents were pleased with this because it was a tradition that young men and women spent time alone with the earth, the animals, and the great spirit. This was good for Turquoise and Warrior because no one would go against anyone's journey with the earth and the great spirit, for this was their heritage. So both Turquoise and young Warrior's story would last a long time. So this was a good thing, although they felt bad that they were telling a lie to their parents and their tribe. But they were happy it worked. They continued to see each other everyday.

Sometimes they would ride their horses all day and other days they would walk them. Although he thought that playing as a child was not fun and pointless, playing games with Turquoise was so enjoyable and fun that that's all he wanted to do. Turquoise and the young warrior even stopped going home and even set up their own camp.

The young warrior would go and hunt during the day and collect firewood by the afternoon. Turquoise would prepare the food during the day. They were so much in love with each other and loved living with each other so much that they forgot about their tribes. After seven days, Turquoise said, "What about our tribes? What are they thinking? Do they think we're dead? We should go back home and stay a couple of days so they don't get worried." Warrior agreed. "We will go home tomorrow and tell them we were on a spiritual journey with the great grandfather spirit, the earth and the animals."

The whole night, the young warrior embraced Turquoise. He held her so tight that the next day his arms were so weak that he couldn't do much with them. Turquoise woke up and Warrior took his arms from around her. As he was looking in her eyes, he told her how much he loved her and told her how beautiful her eyes were as he kissed her eyelids. He kissed her nose and told her how cute her nose was. He kissed her lips and said how gorgeous her smile was and how pretty her teeth were. He said, "You're the love of my life, the girl of my dreams. You're everything I want and I thank the great grandfather spirit for you and for bringing you into my life. She said that she felt the same way. She was so happy that she had found him and that she has fallen in love with him. She felt like her heart would burst open. She said that it felt like her heart wasn't hers anymore and that it belonged to him. And it was his to keep forever. He smiled and was so happy that tears fell from his eyes. Then they began laughing with great joy. They agreed that it was time to go home. They embraced each other, kissed, and then went on their own ways.

As Turquoise started on her way home, Warrior chose to stay and spend the day in the canyons. He began searching for a piece of turquoise as beautiful as she was. He came upon a few pieces that he thought that might be the one, but decided to keep on looking. After all day of searching, he came upon the most beautiful piece of turquoise that he had ever seen. He thought that this would be perfect for the necklace band he would make for her.

The young warrior was about to ask Turquoise to marry him. He picked up the piece of turquoise and started heading home.

It was getting dark and Warrior was tired. When he got home, his parents wanted to know where he had been. He told them that he was on a spiritual journey with the great spirit and the earth. His parents said, "How was your spiritual journey with the great spirit and the earth and animals?" Warrior said that it was wonderful and that he had learned a lot of new things. His parents were pleased.

They asked if he would share with them his adventure, but he told them he was too tired. All he wanted is to go to sleep. He said good night to his parents and they said, "Good night son. We love you."

He said, "I love you too." He slept well that night.

The next day he woke up and started making the necklace.

He spent all day making it. He even went to some elder wemen in the tribe to help him with the necklace. He made it so beautifully that one elder woman said, "Who's the lucky squaw? He smiled and said,

"This is for my friend. There is no lucky squaw." They laughed and said, "Ok. If you say so." When it was finished, he went to his tent and put it under his pillow. Then he went to help around the camp.

His heart was full, his soul complete. He had what every young warrior would always long for . . . a beautiful girl who had given her heart to him completely.

Some of the people of the tribe asked him were he was for those long days and said that they missed him. He said, "I was on a spiritual journey with the great grandfather spirit and the earth."

They asked, "How was your journey?" He said, "It was very good for me. I love to be with the spirit of the earth and the animals. It made me feel as one with them." The young warrior felt bad about telling a lie, but felt good that it worked. After getting some firewood for some of the elders who could no longer get it for themselves, he went to his tent. His mother was preparing some food. She asked Warrior if he was hungry. He said, "Yes, mother.

I'm starving." His mother smiled and said, "Come. Eat well."

Warrior was eating his parents asked him if he was going on another spiritual journey. He said, "Yes. I have one more to go on.

This one is the most important one in my life." His parents asked, "Why is this one so important?" Warrior answered, "Because in this one, I will find myself." His parents were pleased. He was done eating when he said to his mother and father, "Good night. I love you." His parents said, "Good night. We love you, son." As

Warrior laid in bed, he was so happy about asking Turquoise to marry him that he could not go to sleep, even though he was very tired. He pulled the necklace from underneath his pillow, put it on his chest, and began to feel peaceful. He fell right to sleep.

The next morning, he set off to go see Turquoise. When he finally got there, she was also arriving at the same time. They were so happy to see each other that they rushed into each others arms and held each other very tightly. They said how much they had missed each other. Warrior said to her, "Come with me. I have something to show you." They both jumped on his horse and went to a waterfall.

They rode up a hill overlooking the waterfall. There he got her off the horse and sat her down. Warrior told her how much he loved her, how glad she had came into his life, and that he wanted her to be in his life forever. As he looked into her eyes, he said, "Will you be my wife?" With tears coming down her face, she said, "Yes, I will be your wife." Warrior hugged her, squeezed her tight, and then kissed her on the lips. All Warrior wanted was to be in her presence and absorb everything about her. Warrior reached into his pocket and pulled out the necklace band and put it around her neck. With tears of joy coming down her face, she smiled and said, "It's beautiful i will cherish it as long as I live."

Warrior was so happy. He kissed her and said, "I love you turquoise Turquoise said, "I love you, too warrior "What about our families? We'll have to tell our parents and get their blessing."

Warrior said, "Ok. We will go to each other's tribes and get their blessing." Turquoise agreed. They spent the rest of the day together with their horses by their sides they walked back to Sunset Hill where they first met. They sat there and watched the sunset.

Then they went to their camp, ate some food, and went to sleep.

Warrior said, "We will go to my tribe in the morning." Turquoise agreed.

They both went to sleep.

The next morning, they got up and set off to Warrior's tribe.

When they got there, Warrior went to his parents and said,

"Mother, Father, this is Turquoise This is the girl of my dreams.

This is the lady I'm going to marry." His parents were happy.

Warrior's soon-to-be wife said to Warrior's parents, "Hi. My name is Turquoise. I'm from the Apache tribe." Warrior's parents said,

"Your tribe and ours are at war. We have been fighting each other for over fifty years. How did you guys meet? Warrior said,

"Remember when I said I was on a spiritual journey? Well,

Turquoise was my spiritual journey. Since I was 13 years old, I would go to a place I called Sunset Hill and watched the sunset until I was 16 years old. Then one day, I went to Sunset Hill when I saw someone sitting on a horse. I wondered who it was, so I went to go see who was enjoying my hill. That's when I saw the most beautiful girl I had ever seen. I felt something that I never felt before. It felt like this whole time, I was not even alive. I was missing out on so much. I thought to myself: Does everyone feel this way? So you see, it was truly a spiritual journey. So I was not really telling you a lie when I said that I was on a spiritual journey.

I fell in love at first sight. We started talking. She said that she had been coming here since she was 13 years old, but we had never seen each other until we were 16 years old. So you see, the spirit did not let us see each other until we were 16 even though we were so close to each other. So you see, it was meant to be. When we found out that our tribes did not get along, we kept it a secret by saying we were on a spiritual journey which we were sorry for lying to our tribes. But we loved each other too much not to see each other." His parents said, "We love you and because you are our son, we want to see you happy. We bless your decision and wishes, but we have to tell you that we don't know if the tribe would accept your decision. Warrior's mother said, "Your father and I want you to be happy, so whatever happens, just know we still love you both." Warrior's parents hugged and kissed them both.

Warrior went to the chief and when he got there, the chief said, "I knew you both were coming. I had a vision of you two. I say it cannot be. We are from two different tribes that are at war and have been for some time now." The chief said, "Young warrior, you are a good spirit and you mean good, but you need to understand that by marrying Turquoise, you could lose your life.

Your rivals might kill you and because we are at war, I cannot bless your marriage. Forgive me." Warrior was upset, but was so in love with Turquoise, that it didn't get him down. He said, "Okay, I'll just have to leave my tribe and live with Turquoise alone."

So Turquoise and Warrior set off to live their lives. As they were leaving, some wemen of the tribe were giving Turquoise ugly looks. One walked by her and bumped her shoulder. Then one came right at her to hit her with a stick but Warrior stopped her.

The other Indians held her back. She was yelling out, "Your tribe killed my brother! I hate you! "I hate you Warrior and Turquoise got on their horse and left. Turquoise was crying. She was saying, "It's not my fault! It's not my fault. I'm sorry. I'm sorry. It's not my fault.

Warrior stopped the horse, got her off the horse, and held her in his arms. He said, "I know its not your fault. I forgive you for something that you do not know about. I love you so much. I love every tear coming out of your eyes. I love your good heart and I don't mind you crying because it makes me happy that I'm here to hold you. Not only will I be here when you stop,crying but I pray that I could carry the burden of your sorrow." Turquoise said, "Thank you for loving me so much." She stopped crying and then felt a feeling of peace. Warrior's prayer worked. Turquoise looked at

Warrior. He was crying, but Turquoise could not feel bad because Warrior was carrying her sorrow. She tried to talk to Warrior.

She said, "I don't think its fair that I'm happy and you're crying."

Warrior could hardly talk. He said, "I love you so much that I can't stand to see you in pain. I thank the great spirit for answering my prayer." He said, I'm sad, so you won't be." Turquoise said,

"That makes me glad." Though she thought it not fair to Warrior, she could not feel bad. So she made the best of it. She kissed him and said, "I love you, Warrior."

Turquoise and Warrior set off for their camp. They spent the night at their camp. In the morning, they set off for Turquoise's tribe. When they got there, right away they started getting bad looks from the warriors of the tribe. They were on their way to Turquoises parents' home, but they didn't make it. Some of the warriors started gathering around Warrior and Turquoise when one asked Warrior, "What tribe are you from?" Warrior said, "I am from the Cahuilla tribe." That's when one of the warriors hit Warrior in the head. Then about five warriors started beating Warrior. Turquoise started screaming, "Stop! Get off of him!"

But they did not. One warrior looked right into Turquoise's eyes and hit warrior in his head with a rock. Turquoise screamed, "No . . . !

Noooo!" She jumped right into the warrior's path. She said, "Get off of him!" The warriors grabbed her and threw Turquoise back.

She flew and hit the ground. She got back up jumped into the fight.

This time one warrior grabbed Turquoise and told a group of wemen to hold her down. They grabbed Turquoise and held her down. Turquoise screamed, "Please let him go! Please, please!

The chief came out. He said, "Stop it!" The warriors stopped hitting Warrior. The chief saw Turquoise crying. He said, "What's going on here?" One warrior said, "He is from the Cahuilla tribe." The chief said, "Is this true?" The young warrior said, "Yes, I'm from the Cahuilla tribe and I fell in love with a squaw from your tribe."

Turquoise said, "I love him and want to marry him." One warrior said, "What? You'll marry the enemy?!" Another shouted, "Traitor!" The chief said, "Silence! Is this true?" Warrior said, "I am here to ask your blessing. We want to get married." The chief said. "I will not have it!" Turquoise pleaded, "Why . . . why I love him!" The chief said, "Silence!" Turquoise cried. She said, "Well just let us go from this place. Let us go from here." The chief looked at the warriors and waved his hand. They grabbed the young warrior. Turquoise screamed, "No, no, let him go!" Then about five wemen grabbed Turquoise and held her down. She screamed, "No!" They took Warrior on a horse and about five more warriors rode off with him. Turquoise screamed. She was kicking and foughting "Let me go! Get off me! They held her down.

After a few hours, she gave up. She began to weep uncontrollably.

Turquoise was in so much pain she felt like dying. After a few more hours, her mother came to comfort her. She sat there with her.

She said, "Oh, baby . . . oh baby. I'm so sorry. I'm so sorry." She kissed her and said, "Please come inside. Let's go home." She picked up Turquoise from the ground and took her home to their tent. She tried to talk to her, but she wouldn't say a word. She just kept staring at the ground. Turquoise's mother felt so bad for her daughter that she started crying. It started to become sunset when Turquoise heard the warriors coming back from the open land.

Turquoise ran out of the tent to the warriors. Turquoise started gathering rocks. She began to throw them. She hit one warrior in the head with a rock and another in the chest. Her mother came out of the tent and grabbed Turquoise by her arms and held her down.

Turquoise screamed, "What have you done with him?! What have you done with him?!" She screamed out with hate towards the warriors. After awhile, Turquoise's mother managed to bring her into the teepee. She tried to talk to Turquoise but Turquoise screamed, "Shut up!" She was so mad that she sat down and with a mean face looking towards the teepee opening. Her mother started praying for her doughter Turquoise sat there just looking. She waited until the wee hours of the night, then got up, grabbed a horse, got on it, and rode off to go look for Warrior. She could hardly see where she was riding because of the tears coming out of her eyes. She said a prayer, "Please, please, great grandfather spirit. Let Warrior be alive. Please let him be alive. Please, please don't let him be dead."

The sun started to come up. Turquoise was riding all over the plains looking for Warrior. It was now getting to be midday and she still hadn't found Warrior. She got off her horse, knelt on her knees, and started crying. She cried out, "Why? Why did this happen?" I love him. Why, why?" That's when Turquoise heard an eagle screaming. She looked up. It was flying circles around her.

It circled her two times, then went in one direction. She got up and followed the eagle It flew over a hill. Turquoise ran to followed the eagle over the hill. When Turquoise got over the hill, she walked and then she saw something in the tall grass ahead of her. It was Warrior. He looked dead. He was full of blood. She knelt on her knees by Warrior. She touched him. He moaned. He was still alive.

Turquoise said, "Thank you, grandfather spirit. For he is still alive.

She picked him up. And with all her anger and all her strength, she managed to put Warrior on her horse. She took him to their camp.

When they got there, she took care of him. She cleaned his wounds. Then she hand fed him. After wards, Warrior slept.

Turquoise was so angry, but so thankful that he was alive. She did not leave his side. after a few week of takeing care of warrior he began to get better. Turquoise had to do all the hunting. She took very good care of Warrior for she loved him with all her heart. She was so glad that she had him back. She always said, "Thank you, grandfather spirit for saving Warrior life"

After a few week, Warrior started getting his strength back. After a month, he started hunting again. Warrior's leg was broken so he only could hunt so much. But he tried his best. Turquoise couldn't love him any greater. She adored him.

They lived together for six months. Then one day Turquoise'S father sent out a search party to look for Turquoise. The party was

Turquoise's father and four brothers. They looked all day among the open land. Still they didn't see any sign of Turquoise. The sun began to go down. When they saw smoke far over the hills, they went to see where it was coming from. When they got there, they saw that it was Turquoise and Warrior. One of Turquoise's brother's began to go where they were, but Turquoise's father put his arm out and stopped him from going over there. The father said, "We will get her in the morning." Turquoise's father and four brother's waited until the sun started coming up. Then they all went over to their camp. Two of Turquoise's brothers went into their teepee. One more brother went in. Two brothers grabbed Turquoise while the other put a knife to Warrior's neck. They took Turquoise out of the tent. Turquoise realized what was going on.

She started screaming, "No! Leave us alone! Stop it! Stop it!"

Turquoise's brother grabbed Warrior. With the knife to his neck, he brought Warrior out of the tent putting him on his knees.

Turquoise screamed, "No! Leave him alone! Leave him alone!" Turquoise's father said, "I'll give you a choice. If you let Turquoise go, I'll let you live. If not, I'll kill you right now." Turquoise screamed,

"No, don't do it." Warrior shouted, "Kill me! Kill me! I can't live with out her, so kill me! "Turquoise screamed, "No, don't do it!"

Turquoise's father said, "So what will it be?" Warrior said, "Kill me!" Turquoise said, "No . . . no!" Turquoise said, "Warrior, I love you, but I can't live knowing you are dead. So let me go! I can't live knowing you're dead! Let me go! Let me go!" She was sobbing with her head down. Warrior thought about what she said, but was too angry and was being too selfish and said, "Kill me!"

The father looked at his son and nodded his head Turquoise's brother took the blade from his neck and hit Warrior in the back of the head with the butt of the knife.

Turquoise screamed, "No!" Warrior was knocked unconscious.

Turquoise realized that he was not dead, so she stopped fighting.

They took her back to their camp. Warrior woke up. He found himself on the ground. He noticed that they took Turquoise. He wept like a baby. He thought he would die. For the pain he felt was so great he sobbed for hours.

The sun started to go down. He picked himself up and started walking home back to his tribe. He was so sad, he couldn't stop crying when he got home to his parents' tent. His mother saw that he was crying. His mother asked, "What happened?" "They took her from me. They took Turquoise from me forever!" Warrior cried. His mother held him tightly and he cried himself to sleep.

Young Warrior suffered his love for many years and thought that he could never love again. Although there were gorgeous young wemen in his own tribe that captured his eye, he thought:

"What's the use if there is no connection." If there is no striking feeling of love at first sight, it was not meant to be. After experiencing this with Turquoise, other girls just didn't appeal to him, One night, he had a dream and in his dream, he felt pleasant. There was nothing wrong. Everything seemed to be alright in his tribe. He felt good like a void was filled in his life. He felt like he owned something, but not just anything. It felt like nothing he felt before . . . like he owned someone's heart. Then he remembered Turquoise. He began to get excited and he ran. He didn't even stop to get a horse. He just started running. He was running to Sunset Hill where he met

Turquoise in his sleep. His heart started to beat quickly and hard.

He was running faster and faster through the woods. He could see through the woods to where Sunset Hill was. He began to feel weary and he started to slow down. He started to walk as he stepped out of the woods He fell to his knees. He started to remember that he lost her. He started crying and began to wake up.

As he was waking up, he noticed that he had been crying in his sleep. His pillow was soaking wet and there were tears running down his face. He got up and went to start a fire. He said to himself: "I don't ever want to go back to sleep. It was too painful."

He stayed up all night until the sun was coming up. He started to work. He worked all day. Then the day was coming to a end. He began to feel fearful. He was tired and did not want to go to sleep.

He did not know what to do, but was so tired that he said to himself: "I will have to go to sleep sometime. I can't stay up forever." So he went home and knelt by his bed and said, "I don't want to dream about Turquoise anymore." He said it over and over again, "I don't want to dream about Turquoise anymore. He fell asleep saying this and he went into a deep sleep. He saw

Turquoise's face and he tried to wake up. He tried to sit up or to lift his head. He tried and he tried, but felt like a great weight was upon his body. He thought" "If only I could just open my eyes."

He tried and he tried, but he couldn't open them. Then he gathered all his strength and shouted in his sleep. He managed to open his eyelids little by little and slowly he was able to open his eyes.

When he opened his eyes, he noticed that he was moaning in his sleep. He immediately sat up. He was sweating. As he wiped the sweat from his head, he thought to himself that that was the hardest thing that he ever did in his life. He started to cry. He said as he was crying, "I don't want to dream about Turquoise anymore."

After a while, he fell asleep. He dreamed, but of nothing. Then in a dream, he was staring at the stars. It was then when someone grabbed his shoulder. He turned and looked. It was Turquoise.

She was smiling and she was all so beautiful. He started to smile. She said, "Did you hear me?" He said, "No, I'm sorry. What did you say?" She said, how many children do you think we'll have?"

He smiled and said, "I don't care, just as long as they are with you. I don't care warrior said. Turquoise, there is something I've been wanting to say to you . . ." She said, "What is it?" He said, "I wanted to tell you that you're the most beautiful girl in the world and I love everything about you. I love your eyes. I love your hair. I love you from your head to your toes. I love your heart and that it belongs to me. Turquoise, I want you to have my heart." She said with a joyful voice, "I'll keep it forever." Warrior smiled and took her hands, looked into her eyes, and said, "Turquoise, can we sing a song?" She said, "Yes."

And he began to sing a song. He sang, "I have your heart and you have mine together. Our souls are intertwined like the stars and the moon. Our love will shine. Our love is like the air that I breathe and when I'm weak the food that I eat that satisfies my hunger.

The water that I drink to quench my thirst. When I'm thirsty, you're everything I need and desire in my life. I thank you great grandfather spirit for my food, the waters, and the lady in my life. I have your heart, and you have mine together Our souls are intertwined like the stars and the moon. Our love will shine."

Warrior found himself singing in his sleep. He woke up in bed and he realized that he was dreaming. He felt good and at peace. He just enjoyed it. Although he missed her, he did not cry. He just layed there and enjoyed the feeling of peace. He was glad and thankful. It did not hurt and he thought at least it did not hurt. He layed there and thought that he might be able to get over her. He said to himself:

"As long as it doesn't hurt . . ." and went back to sleep.

He woke up the next day feeling better, but he said, "**I** know now that I can't stop dreaming about Turquoise. It won't be as bad if I understand that she's gone and won't be coming back." That's a dream he knew wouldn't be coming true. At least he wished it would, but he knew it would not. Warrior was 25 years old now.

He met Turquoise when he was 16 years old. He knew her for four years. Warrior loved her much but as a young man he realized that although he would never love another like he loved Turquoise, that he must accept the fact that he lost the love of his life and must move on with his life. The dreams continued and Warrior chose to enjoy them and tried to understand as long as he enjoyed them, the pain would not be there and he would not suffer.

Some months passed and Warrior still hadn't desired another, but he didn't want to wait any longer. Then one day Warrior saw a young lady burning some sage. She was praying. Warrior walked over to her and said, "Can I join you in a prayer?" She looked up and said, "Yes," He sat down and looked at her. To his surprise, she was strikingly beautiful. He smiled, but she didn' t. She just started praying. Then Warrior started to pray. He prayed that his heart was completely free from Turquoise. He felt like an Indian giver because he gave Turquoise his heart and now he wanted it back to give it to someone else. This was his prayer. When he was done, he looked at the girl. She was in deep prayer. Then she stopped and looked up. Warrior said, "I'm sorry, but can I ask you what you're praying for?" She said I'm praying for you." Warrior said, "Me?

Why would you be praying for me?" She said, "I know what happened to you. I saw you with Turquoise." Warrior said, "How do you know her name?" She said, "I was there when you were talking to the chief about her tribe." She said, "I must admit that I have never seen anybody so happy together than you and Turquoise. I mean you can see this glow around the both of you. It was so beautiful that even though Turquoise was from the other tribe that ours didn't get along with, I did not hate her, but I loved her. For she loved you and saw past our differences. You both inspired me to look past the horizon, past the little problems of are world. and challenged me to think bigger than the mountains, than the sky, than the moon" the stars and the sun. Whenever I felt discouraged, I thought of the both of you and was once more inspired. Then I felt sad for what you both might be going through.

That's when I began to pray for you guys both. When you came back home, I saw that you didn't have that glow anymore. You looked so sad that it broke my heart. Where's Turquoise? Did she die? I wanted to ask you what happened, but you looked so sad that

I decided to leave you alone and prayed about it. Great grandfather spirit showed me in a vision what happened to you. He said that you were beaten by Turquoise's people, they took you from her and left you for dead in the open land. And how Turquoise came looking for you and that you almost died. He told me how she loved you so much and you loved her. He also told me how her father and four brothers came and took her from you. So you see, I've been praying that your heart be healed." Warrior said, "I'm surprised. I didn't think that anybody cared. I am so proud of you.

You are a true friend. Thank you for caring and thank you for your prayers." Warrior stood up and with his fist in the air he shouted thank you, great grandfather spirit for my people!" He turned to look at the girl. He said, "Thank you. For you made me proud.

What is your name? She smiled, stood up and said, I am Sage." He shook her hand. They started talking and then they started walking.

They walked through the woods and spent all day talking.

The sun started to go down. Warrior told Sage how he and Turquoise used to watch the sunset. He talked about Turquoise all day and Sage seemed interested and eager to listen to what he had to say. Warrior was shocked that it did not bother Sage that he talked about Turquoise. It did not even bother her, but excited her.

For in her eyes, in her opinion, they were the only ones in love and no one else even knew what they were missing. Warrior said to himself: "Maybe she felt that she might not see what Turquoise and he had. in anybody ever again." And that's what he liked about her.

Warrior said to himself: "This girl is not selfish about anybody, but she worries that she might miss out on the beautiful things in life."

For she did not have to say anything. For Warrior knew that Sage liked him, but not just him. She liked the beautiful things that he carried in his life. He thought about what Sage had said to him. It worried him because now he realized that he had feelings towards Sage. **It** worried him because although Sage liked Warrior, she *loved* life and the beautiful things in it. That's why Warrior was worried. Because if he was not true with himself by acknowledging that he had feelings for Sage, he might lose the chance to be with her. All it would take is for someone to be beautiful and true with their feelings and he will lose her forever. But against his instincts, he played it cool and said nothing. They walked back to camp and said goodnight. They turned and started walking home. Then Warrior turned around and said, "Turquoise! I mean . . . Sage. I'm sorry." Then Sage smiled and laughed. At the same time Warrior said, "I'm glad that I met you and thank you for giving me my pride back." She smiled and laughed. She didn't say anything.

She just turned around and walked away. Warrior stood there and watched her. He did not know what to think. Then he turned and went home.

Sage was so happy that tears were running down her face.

For she knew all that she needed to know. Warrior liked her, but she did not know how much. Now she knew that it could be possible that Warrior one day would fall in love with her because he called her Turquoise. Although most girls would get mad and jealous, this made Sage happy because she might be a part of the beautiful things in this world. She was so glad and happy. She said a prayer that night. She lit some sage and said, "Dear great grandfather spirit, I thank you for Warrior and thank you that I can be a part of his life. Thank you, thank you." Sage went to bed.

Meanwhile Warrior just went to bed. When warrior was sleeping that night, he heard a voice. The voice said, "Warrior, don't let the good things in life pass you by. Don't let the good people in your life get away from you. For you will miss out on the good things in life."

Warrior did not wake up until the next day, but he was well aware of the voice he heard and thought of Sage. He got up. He walked fast to Sage's teepee. Sage was making a basket. Sage looked up and saw Warrior standing there. She didn't say anything. She just kept on making the basket. Warrior started to say something.

Sage looked up at him. He caught himself. Before he spoke, she saw that he was trying to say something. She did not pressure him. She just kept making the basket. Warrior thought he would tell her that he heard a voice the night before, but did not want her to think that he was saying this because of the voice he heard. He felt she deserved the truth . . . that he hade feelings for her. So he said, "Sage." She looked at him. He said, "I think you're very beautiful and I thank you for seeing past the little problems in the world and that you embrace the beautiful things in life. You make me proud to know you and I want to be a part of your life." Sage stopped working on the basket. Sage began to talk. Warrior sat down right away.

Sage said, "Although I know you will never love me the way you loved Turquoise, I'm alright with that. I'm just happy to be a part of your life and for you to like me. It's like a gift from God. I'm so glad.

So yes. I want to be with you." Warrior was happy. He thought about what she said about how he would not love her as he loved Turquoise. He wanted to tell her that he would love her like Turquoise, but felt that he would be lying to her. For she was right.

He could not. So he said to sage, "I'm sorry. If I don't love you like Turquoise, could you forgive me?" She said, Turquoise was your first love. She was your heart. I understand. It's okay and I forgive you." He said thank you and gave her a hug. Then he gave her a kiss. They began a relationship that was a friendship and admiration of each other. They spent each day doing fun things, but it was clear that Warrior wanted to start a family because that's all he would talk about. Warrior thought about it, but didn't know how to ask her about having children, until Sage just came out and said, I'll have your children. I'll have as many children as you want.

That's when Warrior said to Sage, "Will you marry me?" Sage was happy with tears. She said, "Yes." They got married. Warrior and Sage were making love, but since Warrior got the okay, they started making passionate love. Warrior was very happy and began working very hard preparing for his family. He could wake up one day and tell everyone about his son. To be a family . . . to be a father . . . to him . . . this was the happiest thing.

Nine months later, out popped Warrior's first son. Warrior held a ceremony with plenty of sage burning" plenty of prayers plenty of food, plenty of songs and dance. Warrior danced all day and all night. He praised god for his son with his dance. The longer he danced, the more he was grateful for his son. He danced until the sun came up. Then he went to his tent and knelt by his baby and kissed him all over and over and said, "Your name will be Warrior like me." His baby smiled. The other fathers in the tribe became very jealous and asked him what he had that they did not.

The young warrior would look them in the eye and said that he did not know. A year later he had another child, a baby boy. His name was Hatchet. And the year after that, another child, a baby boy his name was Root.

He had a child every year for five years: two baby girls, Sage and Prayer. After five years of great happiness, there was a smoke signal from another tribe. This caused the chief to send some of his warriors to see what the smoke signal was all about. The chief chose the young warrior as one of the men to go and see about the signal. When the chosen men arrived at the other tribes territory, they were welcomed and taken to the chief of their tribe. The chief told them that they received news from other tribes that there were very large canoes with pale people that spoke in a language that they couldn't understand coming to there land. The chief told the warriors from the other tribes, "We'll have a pow-wow, then leave in the morning. There was plenty of food and drink. The warriors were called around a fire. They sat around the fire. They ate food. then The chief took his cup, drank from it, and passed it around to the warriors so that they all could drink from it. One after another, they drank from the chiefs cup. It was a tea called peyote. The chief said that when an Indian is lost, he must finds himself. We are lost. We need to ask great grandfather spirit what we should do . . . what's going on. The warriors stayed up all night dancing around the fire.

Some warriors had visions, others did not. Young warrior did not.

The sun was coming up. The warriors were still dancing around the fire. The chief came out to the warriors. The warriors stopped dancing. The chief of the tribe asked if any of the warriors had a vision. One of the warriors said that his vision told him that they were people of a great persecution and were running from their persecutors. They were trying to get away from their previous life and start a new one on our lands. Another warrior said that his vision told him that these people were of a great sadness and were starving, dying, and being killed by their chief. His teepee was so big that more than 100 people lived in it. Another warrior's vision showed him how their chief would cut these peoples heads off if they stole a little piece of food and that they were starving. The Indian chief stood quiet and then said, "Thank you great grandfather spirit for these visions." The warriors had their heads knelt down, then raised their heads. The chief said, "You shall go and see these people. Find out all about them. Then return and tell us about what you have seen."

So they set out to see if this was true. When they got to the beach, the young warrior stopped. His heart began to beat very quickly and he felt faint. He did not know if he was dead or imagining it. He was seeing his dream as a little boy. He had to sit down and watch the other Indians interact with these people of his dreams. He could not understand how you could dream about things that had not happened yet. He became very frightened. He thought: "Do we have no control over our lifes or did we already live life once and then live it over again, seeing parts of our life?" He thought: "What's the point?" He was very confused and disappointed that he might not have control of his life. He slowly regained his strength and returned to tell the tribe what he had found out about the strangers. As young warrior was riding back to his tribe, he thought: "If I put my heart and soul into working on something, it wasn't worth it because it was going to happen anyway." He said, "I thought my life was mine and what I do with it is up to me." He felt that he had no control. He felt if he did something, it already happened. He thought: "Why was I even born? What is life? I don't want to be controlled? I want to be in control of my own life. It's mine. It belongs to me." He felt _like d_oing nothing. He did not even want to ride his horse. He just let his horse wander off. He thought the _only_ way to have control is to do nothing.

At the end of the day, his horse began to get tired. The horse just knelt down with Warrior still sitting on its back. Warrior got off. He did not even want to eat. He didn't drink. He did not even take care of his horse. Good for the horse, there was a creek nearby with some tall grass. The horse went to drink out of the creek and eat some tall grass. Warrior laid down and went to sleep.

The next day, Warrior woke up. His horse was by his side. He did not want to do anything. So he went back to sleep. After a while, he thought he at.least should go back to tell his tribe and complete his mission. So he got up, got on his horse, and rode off.

He didn't know which direction he was going and he did not care.

Warrior did not eat nor drink anything after five days of wandering.

His horse managed to get him back to his tribe. When he got there, some of his people ran to him. They got him off the horse. The chief was nearby. He was watching. He just put his head down and went back into his tent. They said that he looked like he was dead.

His face had no life in it. His lips were dry as leather. He was skin and bones. They got him off his horse. His eyes were open, but he said nothing. He had no strength. They took him to Sage. When

Sage saw him, she did not even recognize him. She hand fed him.

Then she washed him up. She tried to talk to him, but he did not say anything. He closed his eyes and went to sleep. Sage began to cry. Warrior's son was playing when he heard one of the children say, "Your father is back from his mission." Little Warrior ran home. When he got there, he did not recognize his father. His mother was crying. He said, "What's wrong, mother?" His mother said, "It's your father. He's sick. He hasn't eaten for days." Little

Warrior said, "Why not, mother?" She said that she did not know.

Little Warrior walked up to his father and knelt right by him. He bowed his head and prayed. He asked great grandfather spirit to give him back his father. Then he got up and went back to play.

Sage got some sage out, burned it, and began to pray. She said,

"I don't know what has happened to my husband, but great grandfather spirit, please give him back his strength so that he can be a father to his children and a husband to his wife."

The next day, Warrior opened his eyes. Sage did not leave his side.

She told him, "Welcome home. I missed you. I was praying for you the whole time." She said, "What happened to you?" He closed his eyes. She saw that he was going through something. He opened his eyes and she did not ask him anything else. She kissed him on the cheek and whispered in his ear, "I love you." She kissed him again.

She layed there with him and then she got up, got some food, and hand fed him.

This went on for a week. Then one day, Sage was lying next to Warrior and Warrior grabbed a hold of Sage. He held her tight and began to cry. He said, "Sage, I do love you like Turquoise. I do. You're the mother of my children." Sage's heart stopped. She thought he would never say that. She had never been happier.

Warrior said to Sage, "Something happened to me. I am not the same." A tear fell down Sage's face. Warrior said, "Pray for me."

Sage said, "I would never stop praying for you." Warrior said,

"What has happened to me, what I'm going through, is hard to explain. All I can tell you is that I'm very sad and weary. I need your help." Warrior said to Sage, "I'm losing my will to live." He said, "I feel like I'm dead . . . like I'm not even here . . . Although I have you and my beautiful children to live for, I still feel this way.

I'm sorry, but just keep on loving me." She said, "I'll always love you and never give up on you." Warrior began to sigh. He said,

"I love you, Sage. I love you." He went to sleep.

The next day, Warrior got up and went to sit under a tree. He just sat there. His children would go and pull on his arm. They would say, "Play with us, daddy! "play with us But he would just sit and stare.

He sat all day. He wouldn't even eat. Sage would, from a distance, watch Warrior. She would cry, but then said to herself: "I have to be strong for Warrior and my children. Then she stopped crying.

The day was coming to an end. It began to get dark. Sage felt like crying, but fought it off. "I can't! I can't! I must be strong. Don't cry . . . don't cry, Sage . . . don't cry . . ." she said to herself. As she walked up to Warrior, grabbed him by the arms, picked him up, and walked him home. She sat him down and hand fed him. If it wasn't for Sage hand feeding him, he would not have eaten at all. This broke Sage's heart. She wanted to cry, but would tell herself, I have to be strong for my family. So with all of her strength, she would fight off the tears. But late at night was when she would not fight off her tears. She thought of the waterfall and let it all come out.

She tried to not let her body convulse from the pain. She did not want Warrior to know that she was crying for fear that he might lose hope.

Each day, Warrior would get up and sit under the same tree.

Sage would go and hand feed him. One day, Little warrior went up to his father and asked him if he could teach him to fish with the spear. Warrior did not speak. He just stared. Little Warrior said,

"It's okay, father. We don't have to go." He knelt over and gave him a hug and said, I love you, father. No matter what. **I'll always** love you." He gave him a kiss on the cheek and went on playing.

Sage saw this from a ways and ran off into the woods so no one would see her. For this was something that she could not hold in.

She wept. When she was done, she dried her tears off and went back to her teepee to fix Warrior some food. After she was done, she went to go feed Warrior. She hand fed him. When she was done feeding him, she went back to her tent. There were five more warriors from their tribe that went with young warrior on his mission. It had been days and they still hadn't returned. The people of their tribe were worried about what has happened to them.

The people were respectful of young warrior's condition but were anxious to know what happened. Some people of the tribe approached the chief. They said, "Young Warrior has not been the same. He does not talk. He doesn't even play with his children. We do not know what has happened to him and the other warriors. Chief, what shall we do?" The chief said, "Wait for the other warriors to come back." On the 10th day, the other warriors came back to tell them about their mission. They told the chief and the people of their tribe about the strangers. They told of a people of no skin color that they had very big canoes. That they came from a very far away land and that they wished to live among us and share our lands.

They were friendly and kind. They set up camp near the shores and beaches. "We shared a meal and traded gifts some Indians from the tribe nearby stayed with the new people," said some of the warriors. "As for the rest of us, we all left to return to our tribes to tell of what we saw." The people of the tribe were lost and didn't understand how there were other people in the world besides them.

How big could the world be? They thought that they were the only ones and that the world was as big as their lands. This opened their eyes to so many different things. They asked, "What has happened to Young Warrior?" The other warriors said that they did not know what had happened to him. They said that he had become faint and did not walk with them to the new people and that he left that same day. "We were all wondering what had happened to him. Is he all right?" asked the warriors. That's when Sage said, "No, he has not been the same. He does not talk. He won't eat. He won't play with his children. He just sits and stares all day long. One warrior said,

I'll pray that he will get better." The chief went back into his tent and said nothing. The people were silent. The warriors went to their families.

The next day, the warriors went to go see the young warrior.

They saw him sitting under a tree. They went over to go talk to him. They asked, "What has happened to you? What is the matter with you?" He said, "Nothing," He just stared. They sat with him all day. They saw how Sage hand fed him. Sage told them that

Warrior told her that what had happened to him made him very weary and sad, and that he was losing his will to live. The warriors did not understand. They told Sage when they got to the beach,

Warrior became faint, collapsed, and that he looked very frightened like he saw some bad spirit. "He sat there and watched us interact with the new people. He did not move. Then right before night fell, he was gone." the warriors said. They did not know what was wrong with him. They hoped he was all right. Sage told them that this had brought her great sadness, but Warrior asked her to be strong for him. "I have been praying everyday for him to get better." The warriors told Sage that they would pray for him, too.

The next day, the chief told the people of the tribe they will live in peace with the new people. "We will go on with our lives and not let this change anything," he said. The people went back to living life as if nothing had happened. It was easy for the people of the tribe to do this because they did not see these new people. But as for the other warriors, they could just not forget what had happened. They could just not forget these new people. They could not stop thinking of them. They tried their best, but could not.

However, they would obey what the chief said and tried their best to live their lives like before.

After a year had passed, the young warrior was sitting under the tree. He was seeing his children playing. He thought: "What am I doing? What do I care? All I ever wanted in life was a family and I have that." He remembered how much he wanted a family and how much he wanted to raise his children. He began to smile. He soon became his old self again and put everything else aside. He got up, walked. over to all his children, and gave them a bear hug. His children were laughing little Warrior said. "We knew you would come back to us, father. We prayed everyday. We love you and are happy. We thank the great spirit that you're back." Warrior began to cry. He said, "I love you, my children. Thank you so much for praying for me." Sage walked up and saw that Warrior was with his children. She began to laugh. She was so happy. She ran to them and they were one happy family again. Warrior grabbed his children and took them under the tree that he sat under for so long.

Sage followed. They all sat down. Warrior began to tell them how sad he was . . . how he had tried to come back, but he was so depressed he couldn't. He told his children how he dreamt of the new people when he was a little boy and when he got to the beach he was seeing his dream as a little boy. This frightened him. He could not understand how you could dream of something that had not happened. He told his children that he felt that life was not worth living because all we have is our lives, and if our lives don't belong to us, then what's the point? What was the point of doing something if it already has happened. He just did not feel like living. But now he sees that although we might have lived before and just living again, at least he can re-live raising his children.

So you see, l love you guys and I just wanted to experience you again." The children did not fully understand, but they understood that they loved their father and said, "We love you, too and are happy you're back. Sage kissed all her children and said I love you. Then she kissed Warrior and said, "Thank you for coming back to us." They sat under the tree while Sage went to go get some food to eat. When she got back, they ate and sat under the tree all day hugging, kissing, and talking to each other until the sun went down. They all got up and went to their tent. The children had their father back that night. Their tent was the loudest tent in the camp. They stayed up until late night then They went to sleep. the next day. Warrior woke up, got little Warrior up and said, "I'm going to teach you how to fish with the spear." Warrior and Little Warrior went to the river. Warrior broke off some branches from a tree.

He showed Little Warrior how to make a spear. He said, "Do what I do." Warrior stepped into the river. Then when he saw a fish. He stabbed the fish with his spear. He counted five fish on one spear.

Little Warrior counted two. They spent all day fishing. Then they went back to camp. Little Warrior told his mother that he learned how to fish with a spear. He was so happy. The next day, he spent time with all his children: Little Warrior, Hatchet, Root, Sage, and

Prayer. They spent all day playing, laughing, and hugging each other. He began working hard on being a father agean

Five years passed and there was word of fighting between the new people and other tribes over the land and territories. The young Warrior did not want to listen or give it much thought. He just wanted to love his children and to be a good father to his family. That was all that he wanted in life. Some of the warriors from the tribe went to the chief and said, "What should we do? Should we prepare for war?" The chief said, "No. We should not let this bother us. We will live as always." The warriors were confused. They did not know why the chief was just ignoring this.

They were worried, but they obeyed the chief. They went on as usual . . . living their lives as always.

A few years later, Warrior was startled by a loud bang. He looked to the sky and it was clear. It was not rain and it was not thunder. Then there was another louder bang. A tepee exploded and there was fire. What was happening? warrior looked at the horizon. It was the people of his dreams . . . . hundreds of them! It was clear to warrior that they were here to fight. The warriors began fighting but it became clear that there were too many of the strangers. The warriors fought to defend themselves the best they could, but they were being killed. Some of the warriors gathered as many children and wemen as they could and with the chief they ran. The young warrior fought bravely to defend his family and his tribe. He was wounded and left for dead. The young warrior was dying and blacked out. When he came to his senses, everything was ominously quiet. He realized that he was not dead, but was badly wounded. He began crawling slowly. Warrior made his way from body to body hoping that he would not find his family. He saw Sage and then his children all laying dead. He began to weep and turned toward! the darkened sky shouting, "Why me?!

Why me?!" Then he passed out again. Some of the surrounding tribes came to bury the dead and thinking that warrior was dead, picked him up from the ground. He moaned. They realized he was not dead and they laid him down and began to clean his wounds.

They took him back to their tribe and cared for him.

Slowly Warrior began to regain his strength and after a few months, he was much better. He realized what had. Happened, but it was very hard for him to believe that his entire family was gone . . . that he was the sole surviving member of his tribe left.

His wife, his children, and his tribe were all gone. At last he believed that they were gone forever. He became very sad and thought about taking his own life. He went back to the place where everyone was killed and relived the horrible slaughter of his tribe and family.

Warrior went to where his teepee, stood, and took out his knife.

He knelt down and held the knife in the air ready to stab himself and die, but something happened. Before he could end his life, he became very angry. The anger burned into his brain and he left to fight for what was left of his way of life. Some warriors followed him and they joined the others fighting the new people. Young Warrior became a chief of a war party. Every warrior listened to what he said and obeyed his commands. Some warriors from Turquoise's tribe came to join the war party. They recognized that young warrior was the chief of the war party. They went and knelt down before him and asked his forgiveness for what they had done to him. Young warrior recognized one of Turquoise's brothers.

Warrior asked, "How is Turquoise? Is she married?" The brother said that she was dead. "The new people ambushed us one morning.

We managed to fight them off, but a lot of our people were killed, including Turquoise and my father." This added to Warrior's rage and anger. The young Warrior now was a chief of a war party. He began to do what the white people had done to his people . . . kill as many as he could. The young Warrior thought that by killing them, it would make him feel better. But it would not bring his wife and children back or his tribe. He felt that was all that he had left . . . revenge!

One day the young Warrior and his war party were riding their horses through the canyons when the young warriors war party was ambushed. Young Warrior saw Indians from other tribe helping the new people fight. Young Warrior and his war party of

50 were fighting them off. He thought they could win if it wasn't for the Indian traders helping the new people. He was losing. He called for his party to retreat. They managed to get away from the fighting. Young Warrior lost 25 warriors of his war party because of the ambush. That day it broke the young Warrior's heart that his own people were helping the new people kill them off. He could not understand how his own people could help the new people kill off their own. This added to his anger. The war party was fighting for their land and for their way of life. After years of fighting, it seemed there were too many of them already here. And there were

too many warriors dying. It seemed so hopeless that many tribes were stopping the fighting and letting the foreigners have the land.

Many tribes joined the new people and helped them fight the warriors. But the young Warrior would not stop nor would he stop until they were dead . . . or he was dead.

A year passed and the chief of the young Warrior sent word that he wished to see him. So he set out to see his chife and when he got there the chief said, "I wanted you to come here so that I can share something with you. When you were a young boy you came to me with a dream and asked me what it meant. I told you that you should forget the dream. I forbade you to talk about the dream to anyone. I had the same dream when I was a little boy. Hearing your dream made me know that my dream was real. It scared me and I told you to not talk about it. I knew what your dream meant all along. I knew that foreign people would come and conquer us, but I said nothing to anyone." The warrior said, "Why didn't you stop the killing? You could have stopped all this and you did nothing."

He took his knife out of his pouch and held it to the chiefs throat.

He was ready to kill the chief, but before he could kill the chief, he suddenly became weak and collapsed. He began to think of his wife and children and began to weep uncontrollably. The chief said that he had also dreamed of this very moment and if he did not stop crying, he would die of a broken heart. "Please stop crying!

Please stop crying! Let me explain. Let me share my dream so that you will not die and understand. Let me heal your broken heart.

Please let me heal your broken heart. When I was a little boy, I had a dream that there was a nation of many tribes of different colored skins, different colored eyes, different sizes of people, different, *faces* . . . everything different. They were all living together on our land. I did not know what it meant until I had another dream.

Great Father Spirit came to me in the dream and he told me of my dream. He told me the people would be from a faraway place . . . that they would come here to live and in time would develop a nation of many tribes of God's children. This is what life is intended to be. I am asking you if you will give up your land and let this great plan of God happen. It would mean the loss of your land, the loss of your people, and the loss of your way of life. But this is the true meaning of life. Will you help God bring this to pass? I asked you just as I said I would. So now you understand why I said nothing and let this happen." This made sense to warrior and he felt that his broken heart was no longer broken and felt honored that the Great Father Spirit would ask this of him. He felt that he could live with this and the more he thought about it, the better he felt. He began thinking about how he would live his life in a new way.

He said that he would start a new family with a new understanding of life. He would be part of God's plan and that pleased him and made him very happy.—

THE END